Dedicated to Melissa
because we've shared wonderful
times here

Acknowledgements

I thank God for the skill and vision to show His world through my photography. The Schiffer Publishing team provided another wonderful opportunity to share my photography with people across the world. The Mid-Atlantic Center for the Arts, in Cape May, made available excellent historical photos.

Cape May Lighthouse

David Biggy

Schiffer Publishing Ltd

4880 Lower Valley Road · Atglen, Pennsylvania 19310

Other Schiffer Books By The Author:
Lighthouses: Maine to Florida
ISBN: 978-0-7643-3177-0 $34.99

Barnegat Lighthouse Perspectives
ISBN:978-0-7643-3454-2 $9.99

Other Schiffer Books on Related Subjects:
Lighthouses of Cape Cod & The Islands
A. P. Richmond. ISBN: 0-7643-2460-8 $14.95

Lighthouses of the Pacific
J. Gibbs. ISBN: 0-88740-054-X $29.95

Schiffer Books are available at special discounts for bulk purchases for sales promotions or premiums. Special editions, including personalized covers, corporate imprints, and excerpts can be created in large quantities for special needs. For more information contact the publisher:

Published by Schiffer Publishing Ltd.
4880 Lower Valley Road
Atglen, PA 19310
Phone: (610) 593-1777;
Fax: (610) 593-2002
E-mail: Info@schifferbooks.com

For the largest selection of fine reference books on this and related subjects, please visit our web site at
www.schifferbooks.com
We are always looking for people to write books on new and related subjects. If you have an idea for a book please contact us at the above address.

This book may be purchased from the publisher.
Include $5.00 for shipping.
Please try your bookstore first.
You may write for a free catalog.

In Europe, Schiffer books are distributed by
Bushwood Books
6 Marksbury Ave.
Kew Gardens, Surrey TW9 4JF England
Phone: 44 (0) 20 8392 8585;
Fax: 44 (0) 20 8392 9876
E-mail: info@bushwoodbooks.co.uk
Website: **www.bushwoodbooks.co.uk**

Designed by RoS
Type set in Amorinda/Schneidler
ISBN: 978-0-7643-3800-7
Printed in China

History

Like most of the New Jersey shoreline, Cape May Point is an ever-shifting land mass, with sand being maneuvered south and west by strong northern and northeastern currents, from the Atlantic Ocean as well as the Delaware Bay. With constant shifting have come dangerous shoals, making sea travel along this portion of coastline a chore.

Today's Cape May Lighthouse is the third tower constructed on Cape May Point. For more than 150 years it has brightened the paths of mariners entering the northern parts of Delaware Bay, a major trade route to the Delaware River and Philadelphia.

In 1823, the U.S. Congress heard the plea of mariners and constructed a light station at Cape May Point; thus, Cape May Lighthouse was born. That first tower, situated around 1,700 feet from the location of the current tower, was 68 feet tall. It lasted until 1847, when high tides began surrounding it. The site of the original tower now is under water.

A second tower, built about 600 feet south of the current tower, was a 78-foot-tall structure that turned out to be poorly constructed. Ten years later it was replaced by the current tower, a 157-foot-tall conical behemoth compared to the first two towers. It is similar in style to New Jersey's other two conical towers, Absecon and Barnegat, which were commissioned in January 1857 and January 1859, respectively, and built under the supervision of George Meade. Cape May Lighthouse was completed under several supervising officials, including Captain William F. Raynolds, Captain W.B. Franklin and Major Hartman Bache.

After the first tower was threatened by the sea in 1847, and a second tower's poor construction was considered useless in 1857, the current lighthouse at Cape May Point was erected and put into service on October 31, 1859. *Courtesy of the Mid-Atlantic Center for the Arts. Used with Permission*

When the third tower was finished and its first-order Fresnel lens lighted for the first time on October 31, 1859, the top of the second tower was removed and the base of it converted into a storage building, which remained in place until 1981 when it, too, was washed away by the sea.

At that time, the light station at Cape May Point was flourishing and the next year a pair of keepers' dwellings were completed, followed by an oil house in 1893. About nine years later, one of the dwellings was enlarged, as the light station then housed a head keeper and two assistants as well as their families.

Delaware's Cape Henlopen Lighthouse, which marked the southern entrance to Delaware Bay, was threatened by erosion and encroaching seas in 1924. Its lighthouse keeper, Harry H. Palmer, was reassigned to Cape May Lighthouse. Palmer and his family, including his wife, three daughters and a son, arrived at Cape May Point during a fierce storm. Palmer's daughter, Ada, in an article that originally appeared in *Cape May Magazine*'s Fall 2007 edition, told her son, Charles Givens, "We were so seasick and scared that we were all happy to land safely, and start our new life at Cape May Light."

During his first year as keeper at Cape May Lighthouse, Palmer earned $960. Inspection reports from the U.S. Lighthouse Service indicated he was a meticulous keeper who also enjoyed gardening, as several awards from the Cape May County Chamber of

Commerce had proved. Palmer also won the efficiency flag for the Fourth Lighthouse District in 1924 and 1925 for his meticulous work at the light station.

In 1933, the Lighthouse Service electrified the lantern at the lighthouse, and five years later the light was automated, putting an end to the light keeper's job and Palmer's career. The following year the Lighthouse Service was discontinued and the light station was turned over to the U.S. Coast Guard.

During World War II, Cape May Lighthouse fell dark as part of a blackout mandate by the federal government for the entire Atlantic coast, due to the presence of enemy submarines. In 1946, the original Fresnel lens was removed and delivered to the Cape May County Historical Museum.

A rotating aero beacon was placed in the lantern room of the lighthouse.

While under control of the Coast Guard, the lighthouse's lantern room and roof wore down, as did the tower's white coat. In 1986, the Coast Guard leased the property to the State of New Jersey Department of Environmental Protection's Division of Parks and Forestry, which subleased the lighthouse to the Mid-Atlantic Center for the Arts (MAC). In 1992, ownership of the lighthouse was turned over to the State of New Jersey, and since then MAC has been successful in raising more than two-million dollars toward preservation and restoration projects for the lighthouse and its surrounding grounds.

Much of South Cape May, which was originally developed by Philadelphia lawyer J. Howard Weatherby around 1910, is now gone, but what remains is a beautiful and serene shorebird refuge. It has become one of the most popular sites in North America for viewing the fall bird migration. Many species of birds can be seen in the natural areas throughout the year. In the late summer it becomes a haven for people who enjoy watching Monarch butterflies as they migrate through the area and stop briefly to gain their strength before continuing their journey across Delaware Bay.

While shorebirds and Monarchs draw their own distinct crowds, the lighthouse attracts 100,000 visitors per year and continues to be an active aid to navigation. However, the threat of erosion remains, despite a line of jetties that stretch westward from the City of Cape May, off to the east, to the western side of Cape May Point.

Since 1879, when the beach to the east of the lighthouse curved slightly southward into the Atlantic, Cape May Point has lost more than 1,500 feet of sand to erosion. Now the northward indentation from Cape May City to the Point exists. With massive dunes buffering the shoreline, it appears the lighthouse is safe, as its current light — a 24-inch DCB reflector-type lens that projects a light beam that can be seen for 24 miles — shines brightly for both mariners and lighthouse enthusiasts.

Still, wind and sometimes harsh weather continue to beat against the white tower and its lantern. Occasional reinforcement and restoration are required. Those interested in helping the lighthouse to remain standing can climb the lighthouse for a fee and visit the restored oil house, which in 1990 became an orientation center and museum shop. Contact the Mid-Atlantic Center for the Arts (www.capemaymac.org) to learn more and make a donation.

In 1964 the grounds surrounding Cape May Lighthouse became a state park. Today it receives thousands of visitors each year.

Fast Facts

First lighthouse tower built: 1834

    Height: 68 feet

Second lighthouse tower built: 1847

    Height: 78 feet

Current lighthouse first lighted: October 31, 1859

    Height: 157 feet, 6 inches

    Number of stairs to the lantern: 199

    Original lens: First-order Fresnel lens

    Year the light was automated: 1938

    Characteristic: 1 white flash every 15 seconds

    Daymark: White

    GPS Coordinates: 38° 55' 59" N - 74° 57' 37" W

Brick oil house constructed: 1893

Sunset is often a peaceful time
at Cape May Point State Park.

This page:
Winter is a great time to visit the state park and take in the many vantage points of the lighthouse, even between the leafless trees.

Opposite page:
Many trees surround the lighthouse, providing some interesting views of the white tower.

While walking amid the multiple levels of the bird observatory within Cape May Point State Park, it's easy to catch a glimpse of the lighthouse between spindles.

The beach surrounding the lighthouse allows for many great views of the tower and the summer retreat building that is St. Mary-by-the-Sea, the former Shoreham Hotel.

The architecture of St. Mary-by-the-Sea provides a perfect foreground to the lighthouse when viewed from the southern beach.

Whether from the beach to the east or from behind some of the brush along Lighthouse Avenue, Cape May Lighthouse generally stands out.

This page:
Because the state park is home to a large bird refuge, bird houses abound as Cape May Lighthouse towers above.

Opposite page:
Sunrise in the winter offers its own version of unique views of the lighthouse, especially within the wetlands that surround it.

Puddles in the driveway at the entrance to the state park reflect the white tower and red lantern of Cape May Lighthouse.

Some sunsets,
especially those during
the late fall, cast a
warm glow upon the
lighthouse.

Not only can sunsets
at Cape May Point
be stunning, but also
the reflection of the
lighthouse's lantern in
the nearby wetlands.

This page:
Whether from the eastern observatory deck of the state park or a beach access path on the southwestern side of Cape May Point, the lighthouse is always visible.

Opposite page:
Inside the lighthouse, restoration work over the years includes polished wood leading toward the lantern room. Brickwork on the interior wall has provided a place to commemorate visits by those who sought to be remembered.

This page:
While walking the streets to the south and west of the state park, Cape May Lighthouse can be seen peaking through vantage points, including the porches of many homes.

Opposite page:
The modern light, known as a DCB-224, delivers a beam that is visible for more than 20 miles at sea. The view from the top of the lighthouse offers some of the Victorian architecture of Cape May Point, particularly St. Mary-by-the-Sea.

Planes with banner advertisements trailing behind often can be seen flying by the lighthouse, particularly in the summer.

At one time, Cape May Lighthouse was lighted by a first-order Fresnel lens.

This page:
During World War II,
Cape May Lighthouse
fell dark as part of
a blackout mandate
by the federal
government for the
entire Atlantic coast,
due to the presence of
enemy submarines.

Opposite page:
Some days, the sky
surrounding the
lighthouse can be
dramatic, while other
days bright skies
dominate.

This page:
There is no shortage
of vantage points for
those seeking them.

Opposite page:
In the winter, brown
foliage often provides
an interesting contrast
to the white light
tower, especially just
after sunrise.

This page:
When the sun rises in March, it casts a warm glow on the tower from the northeast.

Opposite page:
Dune grass and fences are a signature of shore life, and there are plenty of both surrounding Cape May Lighthouse.

This page:
While porthole windows were used in conical towers to help light the area just below the lantern room, registers were a mechanism to control the flow of air to the original oil lamp in the lantern room.

Opposite page:
The lantern room of Cape May Lighthouse has 16 windows to help protect the light, while the tower itself has 4 windows — one each at the southern, eastern, northern and western points of the compass.

Cape May Lighthouse stands 157 feet, 6 inches high.

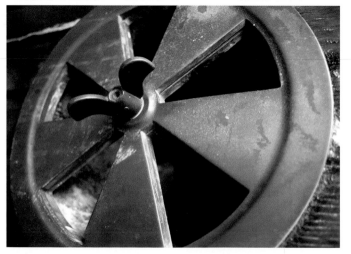

This page:
The oil house was built in 1893 and currently operates as an orientation center and gift shop.

Opposite page:
Crosses abound atop several Victorian structures to the south of Cape May Lighthouse.

The wetlands to the east and north of the lighthouse offer many scenic views.

Plenty of foliage and flowers in varying colors make colorful foregrounds.

Some evenings the summer sun sets and yields to the brightness of Venus behind the light's beam.

This page:
Depending on the vantage point, green cactus-like plants growing around Lighthouse Pond to the north appear taller than the lighthouse.

Opposite page:
Cape May Point State Park is home to Cape May Lighthouse as well as a nature center and massive bird refuge visited by thousands each year.

WELCOME
TO
CAPE MAY POINT
STATE PARK

Cape May Lighthouse
has cast its light for
more than 150 years.

Winter is a quiet time
in Cape May Point.

This page:
Gulls are among the many shorebirds that utilize Cape May Point State Park as a home base.

Opposite page:
Just after sunrise and before sunset, Cape May Lighthouse can be viewed from many angles and still portray a stunning presence.

In March the mornings are full of folks walking the beach to the east of the state park who take in the view of Cape May Lighthouse towering over the landscape.

This page:
Reflections in small bodies of water are in abundance around the lighthouse.

Opposite page:
Whether in a boat on the Atlantic Ocean or Delaware Bay, the Cape May Lighthouse is a magnificent presence along the extreme southern New Jersey coast.

The white tower of
Cape May Lighthouse
can be seen between
trees and shrubs and in
many reflection points
throughout Cape May
Point State Park.

Two of the most picturesque structures in Cape May Point are the lighthouse and St. Mary-by-the-Sea, a sprawling retreat complex.

This page:
Several species of geese make their homes in Lighthouse Pond to the north of the light tower.

Opposite page:
The observatory deck to the east of the lighthouse can provide a different view of the tower, and when nobody's around in the wintertime even the parking lot offers a unique perspective.

One of the trails on the north side of the state park brings visitors to the bird blind on the eastern side of Lighthouse Pond.

This page:
Rapidly growing foliage in the summer delivers vibrant color and interesting perspectives of the lighthouse.

Opposite page:
As a summer day approaches sunset, the marks of many visitors to the beach are evident east of the lighthouse.

Tall grasses surrounding the light tower are hiding places for many species of wildlife that live at Cape May Point State Park.

This page:
Cape May Lighthouse can be seen between the cracks and crevices of acres of foliage from within the state park.

Opposite page:
The lighthouse, with the help of restoration work over the years, has sustained harsh winters at Cape May Point. Dune grass is cut down every year to help it flourish the following spring.

This page:
The presence of Cape May Lighthouse, whether at sunset or at midday, has provided a sense of hope to mariners and visitors for many generations.

Opposite page:
When early spring days provide rain, a reflection of Cape May Lighthouse can be found just about anywhere at Cape May Point State Park.

This page:
Foggy days at Cape May Point occur late in the spring, as air temperatures soar and water temperatures remain cool, yielding a bland sky behind the light tower.

Opposite page:
Depending on the angle of the sun relative to the lighthouse, photographers sometimes will be greeted by the image of rainbow-colored rays.

Each day the sun sets at Cape May Point State Park, it signals the end of another day in the life of Cape May Lighthouse and many of the shorebirds that live nearby.

Photographer David Biggy.
Photo by Melissa Biggy

About the Author

David Biggy, a professional sports journalist, writer and photographer, has lived in Barnegat, New Jersey, since 1999. Growing up in North Jersey, David's passion for photography developed during his teen years and grew along with his interest in journalism during his years at Ramapo College of New Jersey.

He first photographed a lighthouse in 2000, and over the next four years he and his wife visited another dozen lighthouses in New Jersey and Maryland. In 2004, to sell his photography, Biggy's Photos, Etc. was born. Since then, David has photographed about 200 lighthouses and lightships along the East and Gulf coasts and the Great Lakes.

David's approach to lighthouse photography is simple. If he sees a shot he likes, he shoots it with whatever lighting and conditions exist. He uses natural props—such as trees, shrubs, birds, clouds, other architecture and landscapes or seascapes—to capture an appealing scene. Visit www.biggysphotosetc.com.

His books, *Lighthouses: Maine to Florida*, (2009) and *Barnegat Lighthouse Perspectives*, (2010) are available on his web site, from the publisher, and where good books are sold.